Orpheus and Eurydice

Edward Eaton

A Verse Drama

Published by
Dragonfly Publishing, Inc.

Orpheus and Eurydice
A Verse Drama

Paperback Edition
EAN 978-1-936381-48-7
ISBN 1-936381-48-6

Story Text ©2012 Edward Eaton
Jacket Design & Illustrations ©2012 Dragonfly Publishing, Inc.
Dragonfly Logo ©2001 Terri L. Branson

"Death of Eurydice" [Painted in 1861 by
Jean Baptiste Camille Corot (Public Domain)]

Published in the United States of America by
Dragonfly Publishing, Inc.
Website: www.dragonflypubs.com

TABLE OF CONTENTS

*This work is dedicated to my wife, Silviya,
and to my little man, Christopher.*

Sine quibus non

Dramatis Personae

EURYDICE: A young bride

ORPHEUS: Her husband, a singer

DEMON 1: A tormentor

DEMON 2: Another tormentor

HADES: King of Hell

PERSEPHONE: Queen of Hell

SCENE 1:
Eurydice in Hell

EURYDICE wakes alone on an empty stage

EURYDICE
Orpheus! Orphe—

She looks around her.

Where are the trees? The bright sun
Which warms the morning?

Where is the grass? The
Birds who sing in their
Leafy nests so high?

The stream by which we
Played and danced beneath
The warm setting sun.

Husband? Love? Where is
Your bright voice to warm this chill
That embraces me?

Orpheus! Darling!
Don't play with me! Sing and bring
Color to my pale cheeks.

Warm me; tease me, love.
Caress my auburn hair and
Touch my frozen hands.

So cold. Why cold?
Why are my limbs so stiff and
My mind so cloudy?

Mama! Papa! Come
And embrace your angel child.
Laugh and make me smile.

Mama! Laugh, Mama!
Laugh at my little jokes, smile
At my clever wit.

Papa! Papa! Will
Your strong arms and your rough grip
Lift me from the damp?

Husband! Love! When is
Your touch, your gentle caress
To awaken me?

Is there no one? Is
Eurydice so alone
With none to love her?

With none to praise her,
To compare her to the sun,
To 'plaud her bright eyes.

To praise her red lips,
To sing songs 'bout silken hair,
Soft skin, gentle hands.

Is there no such one?
Am I truly so alone?
Am I so alone?

What cold place is this?
Dripping rocks and misty air
Scab my gentle limbs.

Where's Eurydice
Now? Lost within an endless
Fog. Where is she now?

She sees a figure.

Wait! Shadowy one!
Come back! Don't leave me alone.
Gone and fled is he.

She sees another figure.

You, woman! Do not
Go into the dark and leave
Me to lonely thoughts.

You walk right by and
Do not turn your heads to see
The one calling you.

Look at me! See me!
I don't wish to be alone!
I don't wish to be!

See me! Behold this
Form that drew the very gods
To gaze in wonder.

These eyes have given
So many promises and
Caught so many hearts.

This face, so fair it
Would be veiled in many lands,
Is open to th'eyes.

See this flesh, these arms
That embrace, these legs that bring
Such delight to men.

Two DEMONS approach.

Can you walk away?

DEMON 1
I do not see—

DEMON 2
Nor do I.

DEMON 1
Any great beauty.

EURYDICE
You do not see?

DEMON 1
No
Subject for poems, songs, or
Any grand desire.

EURYDICE
Are you blind?

DEMON 1
Why would
I waste my tongue?

DEMON 2

And eyes on
Plain Eurydice?

DEMON 1

I see a lump of
Flesh, like so many others.
Nothing special there.

DEMON 2

Clumpy and soft it
Is. Fragile.... T'would break under
The gentlest caress.

DEMON 1

A rough grip would bend
And mark it. The slightest pull
Would rip flesh from bone.

EURYDICE

My skin deserves the
Gentlest touch.

DEMON 1

Shall we then use
Our teeth and rip the—

DEMON 2

Flesh and tear the skin.
It is no great sin to ruin
Such a useless girl.

Perhaps it would stop
Her whining.

DEMON 1

Perhaps it would
Stop her memories.

EURYDICE
You must be blind not
To see me. The clouds would stop
In the sky to look.

They would fight the winds
Just for one glance. They would hold
Rain from thirsty crops

To shade me from the
Sun, which would burn more fiercely,
To see through the haze

And lengthen the days.
Even Diana wanes in
Envy as her dear

Brother stretches out
His arms to bathe me in his
Warm embrace, while she

Goes cold awaiting
Her turn to drag 'cross the sky,
Her pale dusky cart.

Her brother—

DEMON 1
The sun
Warms both the fair and foul, it
Does not matter which.

DEMON 2
Apollo's lust is
No great compliment.

EURYDICE
You lie!

DEMON 2
I laugh at vain boasts.

DEMON 1
Diana pales not
In envy. She turns her face,
Her gaze, away from

Her brother and his
Prey in humiliation
At his aimless lust.

DEMON 2
Even Apollo's
Loveless rays cannot enter
Here to warm you, child.

DEMON 1
Your vapid flesh will
Feel rougher heat before long.

EURYDICE
I don't need the sun.

I do not need gods
To warm me with their praise. The
Very trees and beasts

Are my friends. They laugh
With me and dance to keep me
Happy in the dark.

DEMON 2
No vegetable love
Can take root in this rocky
Soil, lest it whither.

DEMON 1
Nor little lap dogs,
Nor graceful gazelles will lick
Your cheeks in this place.

DEMON 2
The beasts are fiercer
Here and far more rigid in
Their hungry resolve.

DEMON 1
The weeping willow
Weeps, roses bloom, grass is green.
With or without you.

EURYDICE
I want my meadows,
My streams and hills and flowers.
My pillows of soft

Grass. I was not made
For rocks and for shoal. Gentler
Feet need gentler turf.

To what loveless land
Have I been sent by the sting
Of a tiny snake?

DEMON 1
The tiniest snake
Becomes a great serpent when
Looked at from a tomb.

DEMON 2
Many serpents here
Will no doubt seek you out and
Sting you yet again.

EURYDICE

A tomb? It was the
Smallest prick.

DEMON 2

Was big enough
To bring you to us.

DEMON 1

Welcome to Hell, girl
A place of rabid delights.
There is no love here.

DEMON 2

No need to praise you.
A rough caress sings louder
Than the prettiest voice.

EURYDICE

Not prettier than my
Love's. No voice sings louder and
Fills the hearts of stones

With wonder for his
Subject. No voice can speak of
My beauty with such

Sublimity and
Truth. No love knows how to praise
Any lover more.

DEMON 1

What god is this who
Loves any mortal woman
Thus?

DEMON 2

None I know of.

EURYDICE
He is no god, but
A mortal man envied by
Gods, men, and devils.

Only he can sing
And tell the world how lovely
I am. Even the

Spirits stop their cries
Of lamentation when he
Tells them of my eyes.

DEMON 1
A mere mortal man.
We can quickly cure him of
This dread malady.

EURYDICE
A mere Mortal? No.

DEMON 1
If we torture you, perhaps—

DEMON 2
He will hear your screams.

DEMON 1
Perhaps he will come.
Perhaps he will try to save
His little lost love.

EURYDICE
He would. He would. My
Love would come. Though thick mountains
Hide my voice, he will

See my beauty in
His mind and follow his dreams
And take me from here.

DEMON 1
Bring him. Call him. We
Would welcome his resolve; what
Good sport we would have.

DEMON 2
You could watch us tear
The meat from your mortal love
And learn how to feed.

EURYDICE
He would come!

DEMON 1
Of course.

EURYDICE
He'd rescue me!

DEMON 2
Who wouldn't?

EURYDICE
My love! Orpheus!

DEMON 1
Who?

DEMON 2
Orpheus?

DEMON 1
Did
She say that name?

DEMON 2
Yes, she did.

DEMON 1
We know who he is.

DEMON 2
We have heard of him.
We have heard of Orpheus.
Tell us about him.

EURYDICE
Orpheus is my
Own great love. When I was young
I searched high and low

For anyone who
Could see my beauty and then
Fill my heart with praise.

Many tried. The birds
Whistled beautiful airs and
Danced upon the breeze.

The flowers sought me;
They'd burst fully bloomed from the
Ground to smile at me.

The gods sent brilliant
Flashes of lightning to clear
The darkest of nights.

My dreams were filled with
The music of thunder that
Lulled me in my sleep.

EDWARD EATON

The waves fought the tides
To be to near me, and the winds
Stilled to brush my brow.

But they all failed to
Find the means to honor me.
I remained unmoved.

Then one day he came.
Orpheus; he looked at me.
He raised his voice and

Sang out to the stars.

SCENE 2:
Orpheus and Eurydice

ORPHEUS before
HADES and PERSEPHONE,
King and Queen of Hell

ORPHEUS AND EURYDICE
Behold fair Eurydice!
Behold such beauty!

EURYDICE
That is what he sang.

ORPHEUS
(At the same time)
That is what I sang
When I saw Eurydice.
When I first saw her.

Her bright eyes smiled at
Me and set my heart leaping.
They sparked and shone and

Danced in the sun light
And paled the beauty of the
Morning sky. When the

Moon rose, the stars found
Home in her dark eyes. I could
Not tell the diff'rence

Between her eyes and
The sky; though perhaps her eyes
Were all the deeper.

My Eurydice!
Her smile brought me such joy. Her
Face bright and lively.

The moment we met
She leaped into my arms.

EURYDICE

And
Laughed with joy and love.

ORPHEUS

Into my arms she
Leaped, and I knew then that here
I had found a girl.

A subject for all
My heart, my words, my love to
Sing to the heavens,

And make the valleys
Ring with the most beautiful
Sounds I could dream of.

What glorious tunes
Sprang from my lips, wonderful
Songs worthy of gods.

EURYDICE

He saw my beauty
And loved me.

ORPHEUS

I saw her face
And her graceful walk.

I looked into her
Eyes, was lost within their depths,
I nearly drowned there.

Her dainty feet, her
Gentle hands, her ringing laugh,
Her smiles and gestures.

Here at last was a
Girl, worthy of my greatest
Incomp'rable songs.

I sang and she danced
For me. She played and she rolled
On the grass and laughed

And sang and thrilled and
Loved me. Under the sun we
Lay and laughed and laughed

At clouds. In the night,
We held each other quietly
Counting distant stars.

That was our life. Our
Days of joy and dancing and
Nights of deepest love,

Endless time of joy.
Loving our own music, our
Own dance, our own love.

The gods were jealous
Of our happiness. Songs of
Her beauty galled them.

But Jove's thunderbolt
Could not part us, neither could
Neptune's crashing waves.

We held each other
'Gainst the blistering sun and
Frigid blowing snows.

Her people wept when
I took her to me and they
Sadly missed my songs.

But we had a love.

HADES
We understand you loved.

PERSEPHONE
But
What's to do with us?

HADES
We have all lost at
Love. Hell itself weeps in our
Season of despair.

When Persephone
Herself is dragged from home to
Dance under the sky.

You are not the first
To mourn. You are not the first
To lose your lover.

ORPHEUS
Mine is love without
Compare!

HADES
Greater than my own?
Is her beauty more?

PERSEPHONE
Than Persephone's?

ORPHEUS
My loss is all the greater.
For your wife returns,

Yet mine remains here.

HADES
And here is where she belongs.

PERSEPHONE
Why have you come here?

ORPHEUS
To take my wife home.

HADES
You are presumptuous.

ORPHEUS
I
Am a man in love!

HADES
All men have loved. Why
Is your love so different?

ORPHEUS

So I will tell you.

If Sisyphus will
Stop his wearying struggle,
Though 'twill set him back.

Were Tantalus to
Listen to my words perhaps
They'd quench his longings.

I pray all lovers
Would recall their younger days
Beauty, love and joy.

Hear me! Hear my song!
Know that mine is greater than
All the loves of yore!

HADES

Speak!

PERSEPHONE

Speak! Let us hear!

HADES

How you deserve more than those
Who have lost before?

SCENE 3:
Orpheus' Song

ORPHEUS

Eurydice, my
Lost love. I'm here to find you.
I'm to take you home.

Whatever torments
You feel, know I will take your
Place, your agonies.

For without you, there
Is no blue sky. There's no sun,
No moon, no stars, no.

Without you, all love,
Beauty and happiness flee.
Birds no longer sing.

Flowers fail to bloom.
Deer won't dance, grass isn't green
Fish no longer swim.

Eurydice! Hear
Me! I have come to Hell to
Bring you back to me.

The house, the forests,
Hills, streams, oceans and deserts,
Empty without you.

Your loss has taken
Memories of you but for
The merest shadows.

Your beauty had filled
My world with colors, pulsing
Vibrant lights and darks.

Nights and days throbbed and
Leapt out of the grayness that
Mere mortals live in.

You awakened my
Senses, gave meat to flesh my
Imagination.

Eurydice! Now
You are gone and you have stripped
The meat from the bones!

My now, my then, are
A shapeless, formless jumble
Of Eurydice!

Fair love! Come to me!
I call you! Bring back color!
Bring back light to thoughts!

Bring color! Bring air!
Let my pleasure have joy! Let
My songs have music!

Come to me! My love!
Let love carry love from Hell,
To a sweet embrace!

Let me take you to
The forests, where you can dance!
Let me take you to

The desert, where you
Can coax the water from the
Depths of drifting sands!

Let me take you to
The ends of the seas. You can
Calm the distant storms!

Let me take you to
Apollo's, there to quench the
Sun's fiery tears!

Let me take you to
Jove's darkened clouds to stay the
Mourning thunderbolts!

The whole world mourns you!
Yet only I love you to
Lift my humble voice!

My humble voice lifts
From Earth, to the depths of Hell,
Praying for your life!

Eurydice! Come!

SCENE 4:
The Warning

HADES
(overlapping)
Eurydice! Stay!

EURYDICE
I hear my name sung. Who calls?

PERSEPHONE
I will speak with her!

HADES
And I with him. Take
Heed to what I say, young man
Understand my words

PERSEPHONE
Understand my will.
I shall only say this once.
You are to leave here.

EURYDICE
My husband is here?
I thought I felt all Hades
Shivering.

PERSEPHONE
He's here.

But missed you as he
Sought you. He's on his way out.

EURYDICE
Then I must catch him.

PERSEPHONE
If you can, you must,
For then you can leave with him.

EURYDICE
Then I must go now.

PERSEPHONE
You must find him. You
Cannot leave without him, for
If he leaves without—

EURYDICE
Without me? He won't!

PERSEPHONE
You must return if he should
Miss you before he—

EURYDICE
I'll find him whate'er
Clouds you put before his eyes,
Stones before my heart.

PERSEPHONE
He shall not, cannot
Be permitted to return.
Not while I am queen.

EURYDICE
I swear he will hear;
My cries will pierce the heavens;
My beauty, stone eyes.

PERSEPHONE
Then go and find him
And when you two embrace, think
And remember me.

It was I who made
Stern Hades to soften his
Heart and let you go.

You must remember
And know what I've done for you.

EURYDICE
I shall remember.

PERSEPHONE
So go!

HADES
(overlapping)
So go from Hades.

ORPHEUS
Not without Eurydice!
Not without my love!

HADES
Do not fear; have faith.
I, Hades, won't let you down.
But Persephone—

ORPHEUS
Your most gracious wife.

HADES
—Will permit your wife to leave
Only on my word.

'Cause of her exile
From the well-lit world above
To my darkened home,

She would not want to
Let another, however
Much she is loved, go

To dance beneath stars'
Glitters or to warm herself
Beneath the warm rays.

You have softened my
Heart, so I have offered my
Dear Persephone

A brief respite from
Her marriage bed to stroll once
In brisk winter air.

For that gift, she has
Allowed your dear wife to go
And follow love home.

ORPHEUS
And hand in hand we
Will sing and dance in honor
Of Persephone

As we make our way
To the surface!

HADES
That you won't.

ORPHEUS
Why not give her praise?

HADES

When my wife commands,
Sometimes even the king of
Hades must obey.

You must go to the
Surface. There you will find her,
Your Eurydice.

ORPHEUS

On the surface?

HADES

Then
And only then will you find
Your Eurydice.

Hear me. You must go.
Do not sing. Do not calm the
Torments of my guests,

Nor quench their great thirsts.
Nor stay the whips wielded to
Punish my sinners.

I rule in Hell and
Can judge the dead, but it's death
Herself brings them here.

Do not quiet the
Fierce howls of hound Ceberus.
No songs, no tunes. Go!

Eurydice will
Follow your path to the light.
There you can join hands.

There you can say prayers
In praise of Persephone.
Praise her...if you can.

But do not look for
Eurydice. Let her come
And follow your path.

If you look for her,
If you call out to her, then
She will be snatched back.

Pulled once again to
Hell, to remain dead, never
To see light of life.

One word, one glance, one
Attempt to see or speak, then
I'll have her brought back.

No songs or tunes will
Open the gates of Hell. None
Living shall enter.

Charon won't permit
You to cross the river Styx;
Furies will chase you

From the shores and hound
You from my sacred paths...should
You find a way in.

Nor Persephone
Nor I will receive you in
Hades' dreaded court.

Go! The road to life
Will be treacherous without
Songs to clear the way.

SCENE 5:
The Journey

EURYDICE
Where is he? Where are
You Orpheus? Don't you hear
Your Eurydice?

Orpheus! My love!

DEMON 1
Perhaps he cannot hear you?
Perhaps he's not there?

EURYDICE
Persephone told
Me to find my love along
This road.

DEMON 1
Is he there?

My eyes are stronger
Than yours. I see no living
Being on the road.

I will guide you as
Best I can, as ordered, yet
I beg you rethink

This journey. It can
Only end in great despair.
You will not find him.

The trick to Hell is
In the acceptance. All souls
End up in Hades.

EURYDICE

Yet Hades allows
Me one more chance to be with
My love, Orpheus.

DEMON 1

If that is your will,
Then I will guide you past the
Sinners and the dead.

EURYDICE

I'm not int'rested
In the dead. To Orpheus
Only are my thoughts.

Can you see him yet?

DEMON 1

I have yet to look for him.
I have yet to care.

EURYDICE

Then look. Please look now.
Is that his shadow ahead?
Just before the turn?

Orpheus! Hear me!
Dear Orpheus! Is that you?
Why not turn and look?

DEMON 1

It was not but a
Shadow of life to tease and
Torment damn-ed souls.

EURYDICE

There he is. This time
I'm sure I hear him singing.
My love! Sing to me!

DEMON 1

Is but an echo
Of laughter and happiness,
Of life that once was.

EURYDICE

Who's that on the rise,
Walking towards hope with a
Long and purposed stride?

DEMON 1

Lady, I believe
That's merely a memory
Burned inside your mind.

EURYDICE

What trick is this? Tell
Me if I have offended
Hell's Lord and Lady,

That they would tease me
With sightings and rumors of
Where Orpheus is?

DEMON 1

It can't be a trick.
The goddess told me to guide
Eurydice up

To see that…no wait!
What is that I see up there?
No, not what, but whom?

EURYDICE
Tell me. There is fog
Before my eyes that hides my
Sight. Whom do you see?

DEMON 1
I think I see—I—
There is someone up ahead
Where the darkness starts

To fade, where it meets
The swelling morning sunlight.
Someone travels there

Firm and with purpose.
We shall follow his footsteps
In the drifting fog.

Perhaps he's your love.

EURYDICE
I know he is my husband.
He's going so fast.

Orpheus! Wait for
Your loving wife!

DEMON 1
Sinner's cries
Drown young lovers' sighs.

He cannot hear you.

EURYDICE
But he can sense my presence.
I'm the air he breathes.

How can Orpheus
Not know his great love is near?
He came to Hades

To take me home; why'd
He be on the path to the
Living without me?

DEMON 1
Hades' mind is not
Ours to guess. His great lady
Promised your return.

Do not question her
Decision. But catch your love
As she commanded.

Catch him! The gift of
Life is rarely offered...and
Eas'ly taken back.

EURYDICE
I must catch him ere
He reaches the light of day.
Can we slow him down?

DEMON 1
Perhaps we should run.

EURYDICE
And fall from the path? There is
No bottom in sight.

What does the mist hide?

DEMON 1
Is not your love worth the risk?

EURYDICE

Fly ahead to him!

Fly ahead to him!
Why do you wait here with me?
He might get away!

DEMON 1

I am here to guide
You to the surface. Not to
Carry your burdens.

EURYDICE

The rocks are sharp, they
Shred pretty feet to ribbons,
Should I be bleeding?

Should I approach my
Love covered in bruises? Where
Is great beauty there?

DEMON 1

See him; he moves up
The path and further from Death.
We must catch him soon.

It is said that those
Who move close to life forget
The dead left behind.

EURYDICE

He can't forget me!

DEMON 1

Life has a way. Forgetting
The dead lets them live.

EURYDICE
I am his great love!

DEMON 1
Perhaps he'll sing to others,
Fairer and younger.

EURYDICE
He came to Hades
To bring me home.

DEMON 1
And returns
To the life alone.

Hell is death, dear girl,
And in death all beauty fades,
Becomes a mem'ry.

As unclear as all
The past is, veiled in gray fog
We forget color,

We forget the form,
We invent the details and
Soon the mem'ry fades

To be replaced by
A newer reality.

EURYDICE
Then help me move fast.

Then help guide my feet.
Hades is no place for me.
Beauty demands light,

So that those who praise
Me can see me as the gods
Themselves intended.

DEMON 1
I will guide your feet
For Orpheus moves swiftly
And will soon be gone.

Follow me; we will
Take paths mortal souls cannot
Find and go quickly.

Let us be silent
Move like thought, and like thought keep
Orpheus in sight.

Already he is
Becoming like a shadow,
Drowned by rising light.

EURYDICE
Then guide me as you
Promised and I will keep my
Eyes and thoughts on him.

I will call to him.
Perhaps my echoing voice
Will slow Orpheus.

Perhaps the echo
Of his song will guide tired feet
Quickly on the path.

Orpheus! Hear me!
Beyond that bend! There! Past that
Shadow! There he is!

ORPHEUS
Tell me, Hades' slave,
Does Eurydice follow
Or should I go back?

DEMON 2
You cannot turn back
For Hades has forbad it.
One look—and she's gone.

Her soul, her beauty,
Condemned to vast solitude
No voice to praise her.

Would you damn her? Would
You banish inspiration?
To whom would you sing?

And who would praise her?
What's the point of beauty with
Out admiration?

Eurydice would
Fade and become a shadow.
Who would love her then?

Wait, as Hades bade.
Why wouldn't the gods keep their
Word and send her back?

ORPHEUS
I, but I must know.
Must know if Eurydice,
My Eurydice,

Does she follow? Can
She see the path? If I called
Out would she hear me?

DEMON 2
One word and she's doomed.

ORPHEUS
But why? What is the purpose
Of such strict commands?

What's it to Hades
If I see my love while I
Still walk in death's shade?

Are the gods amused
By such arbitrary rules?
It but tortures me!

DEMON 2
Who would you be to
Question divine will?

ORPHEUS
I can
Not bear not knowing.

Look for me!

DEMON 2
I can't!
'Twould be the same to Hades
Were it you or I.

ORPHEUS
How can I move on?
I must know. I must. How can
You be so relaxed?

DEMON 2
I'm not looking for
My love.

ORPHEUS
Are you mocking me?

DEMON 2
I'm advising you.

Hades has ordered!
Who are you to question him?
You're merely mortal.

ORPHEUS
I am he who spends
His days and nights worshipping
Hades. That is why

I have the right to
Demand he returns to me
That which he owes me.

DEMON 2
The gods owe you naught!

ORPHEUS
The gods owe just return for
That which I give them.

Where would the gods be
Without loyal followers?
We sacrifice to

Them. We pray to them.
We give them our sons, daughters!
They should worship us!

DEMON 2
Do not challenge them.
Are you so confident that
You would beat the gods?

ORPHEUS
I have raised my voice
To the divine. Does he close
His ears to my prayers?

EURYDICE: Orpheus—
DEMON 2: Do you

DEMON 2: Hear?

ORPHEUS: What?
DEMON 2: A soft distant voice.

ORPHEUS: No.
EURYDICE: Orpheus!
DEMON 2: There!

ORPHEUS
Do I hear a voice?

DEMON 2
I think so.

ORPHEUS
Could it be she?

DEMON 2
Stop. Listen again.

EURYDICE
Do you think he heard?

DEMON 1
He's stopped. Perhaps he's waiting.
Call him again.

EURYDICE

Love!

Orpheus! Hear me!
It is I, Eurydice!
Hear my call to you!

ORPHEUS

Is it?

DEMON 2

I fear not.

ORPHEUS

I wish you could see—

DEMON 2

There's none
On this trech'rous path

But you and me and
Shadows dancing on the walls
No one real I see.

But I dare not look.
Move forward. Even Hades'
Words do have limits.

Do not tarry here.
The path has been long, but I
Can see light ahead.

EURYDICE

I know he heard me.
Why does he not stop? Why does
He still move onwards?

DEMON 1

Run faster! Call out
To your husband before he
Reaches light of life!

EURYDICE

It is dark! I—I
Cannot see the path! Husband!
Why will he not look?

What's Eurydice?
Is she forgotten so soon?
What beauty is there

In the life ahead
That makes Eurydice plain?
To whom does he go?

It is I have died
Have awakened in dark Hell
Surrounded by hate

Devoured by shadows,
Mocked by the foulest demons.
All the while alone.

No one to touch her,
To give fair Eurydice
Gentle caresses.

Ev'ry great delight
Turned vile. Who is Orpheus
To abandon her?

What fool is he I
Love? I gave him youth; I gave
Him my beauty, mine!

Can he reject me?
Or is he a phantom, slave
To Hades' humor?

Am I to be led
To the edge of life, only
To be pulled...pulled back?

Is my happiness
Simply a joke to the god?
I must know! Love! Turn!

Face your faithful wife!
Show me your face; prove to me
That you are husband,

Friend, and lover to
Fair and sweet Eurydice,
Loyal and loving.

Show me your face so
That I may know your truth and
Then I'll follow you.

Then I'll follow you.
Follow you to life or death.
Turn into the light!

ORPHEUS

I hear a voice, a
Sigh of pain and loss, drifting
On wind of sorrow.

Should I go faster?
Should I? Will she catch me up?
Demon? Answer me?

Is she behind us?
I fear I am now alone
But for an echo.

Is there nothing, no
Eurydice behind me?
No fell guide's advice?

I see life's light there
Calling to me. If I go
Will she come with me?

EURYDICE
Orpheus! Slow down!

ORPHEUS
I hear but dare not turn 'round

EURYDICE
Take my hand, dear love!

ORPHEUS
I feel a shadow
As cold as ice touch my own.

EURYDICE
It is I, your wife!

ORPHEUS
I know it is she.
I can see her in my mind's
Eye just behind me!

EURYDICE
Take my hand! See me!
Feel me! Touch me! Me, love, love!
I am only here.

Inches from your heart.

ORPHEUS
I can feel her shadow. I
See her loving soul.

I dare not turn 'round.
Is it really she? Does she
Follow as I go?

EURYDICE
It is a joke! A
Cruel joke by the gods. They are
Jealous of beauty.

Damn them!

ORPHEUS
Damn the gods
Who toy with their most loyal
Followers theirs! Oh!

EURYDICE
I run up; the path
Does scab my pretty feet, and
Pull at my hair, and

Scratch at this fine face
That means so much to my love
And his lovely songs.

Why I am tortured
So? Why can't I move faster
On this fearful road?

ORPHEUS
I am near the light,
Near the life, but is she there?
What cruel trick is this?

EURYDICE
Orpheus! See me!

ORPHEUS
I dare not turn! I dare not!

EURYDICE
If I but reach out.

If I can touch him
Even cruel Orpheus
Must then feel my hand

ORPHEUS
To the light. Just a
Little further. Fell demon,
Are you still with me?

Can you advise me?
Tell me where she is? My wife?
Is she behind me?

EURYDICE
Reach Eurydice!
Reach out and let love pull you
To life to heaven.

ORPHEUS

Here I am. The end
Of my journey. Only two
More steps to the light

If I go forward
I cannot return and then
Eurydice's dead.

They will not let me
Again through the gates of Hell.
Already I see

Them, foul guardians
Mocking me as I tarry.
Will they not help me?

Are they laughing? Are
They crying? What's in their hearts?
What are they seeing?

I thought I heard her
Is she lost? If I reach out
Can she take my hand?

Two steps and the gates
Of Hell shall close and then she
Will ever be gone.

Come wife! To the light!
Even Hades must allow
Me to say prayers.

Reach out! Make yourself
Known so I can know and now
Lead you to outside.

EURYDICE
Oh, why has he stopped?
He has heard my voice, my call?
Does he wait for me?

I am here, husband!
Take my hand, lead me from this
Unforgiving place!

*She reaches out and
Takes the hand of Orpheus.*

ORPHEUS
My Eurydice!

EURYDICE
My own! Now that you have me
Let us leave this place.

ORPHEUS
Fairer than fairest,
Divinely beautiful one,
My Eurydice!

EURYDICE
Sing a happy song.
Let us arm in arm, hand in
Hand dance into light.

DEMON 1
Hand in hand, gaze you
And languish and then you part
She returns with me.

EURYDICE
I'll not part from him!

ORPHEUS
I have traveled to the edge
Of light to bring her

From this foul and dank
Hell!

DEMON 2
You must part! Let her go!

ORPHEUS
I shall not leave her!

DEMON 1
Come Eurydice.
Let the denizens of Hell
Enjoy your beauty.

EURYDICE
Unhand me, foul beast!

DEMON 1
Let us taste your flesh, caress
Your skin with rough claws.

We shall tear out hair.
Not blushes, but red blood will
Flush your pretty face.

We will gash your eyes,
Rip your beauty and your soul.

EURYDICE
Let me, let him, go!

ORPHEUS
Don't let go my hand!
Hold on!

EURYDICE
Save me! Orpheus!

DEMON 1
Once more to Hades
You are consigned, damned ever.
Back to the shadow.

EURYDICE
Aaah!

ORPHEUS
What have I done?

DEMON 2
What have you done, you fool? You
Turned before the end.

Gracious goddess queen
Persephone and her dread
Lord, Hades, granted

Life where there was death
Hope where there was but torture
But you had to turn
Farewell, Orpheus!
See your love leave, never to
Life's light again!

Farewell!

SCENE 6:
The Return

ORPHEUS
Stay! Stay! Stay!
What did I do? Why did I
Have to turn and look?

Eurydice! No!
I—you—no! What have I done?
Eurydice! Come!

Hades! King of Hell!
Give my wife to me, my love!
Send her back to me!

Dreaded gates of Hell!
Open again your fiery
Maw to find my love!

Persephone! Fair
Queen of Hell and Hade's love,
Have pity on me!

PERSEPHONE
Your lover is dead.
How shall you go on without
Her face, her form, her?

Without her, songs are
But whispers in wind. They are
No sound, no music.

Her beauty unsung,
Because you could not wait and
Did not trust the gods.

Eurydice is
Unloved in Hades, but she
Will not be alone.

For there are demons
And devils in Hades who
Will comfort your love.

Without you she will
Be prey and love to vultures
Who long to taste her.

What, man, will you do?
How will you save your wife from
Hell's feral lovers?

She's alone. How will
You comfort her? How will you
See her? Protect her?

Will you leave her there
Unprotected? Without friends?
But many hunters.

Go to her. I will
Permit you eternity
With Eurydice.

ORPHEUS
With Eurydice?

PERSEPHONE
To gaze, to look, to love your
Fair Eurydice

Will you trust in me?
Do you wish again to see
Your dear wife's beauty?

Iron is cold to touch,
But hot when pressed 'gainst the breast,
Like a lover's touch.

Embrace the iron.
Hold it to you and dream of
Your eternal joy.

That's right. Right. Hold it
Gently and let it slide, but
Momentary hurt,

And then great pleasure.
Close your eyes and dream of her.
Dream Eurydice.

Dream Eurydice.
Oh great Orpheus, singer
Of songs, dream of love.

Let your voice go. I
Will claim your tongue for Charon's
Fee, but your eyes will

Soon behold your hope
And know Persephone's great
Gift to gentle love

That does make gods wane,
Diminish immortals, give
Even Venus shame.

I take your tongue and
Allow you to see beauty
For eternity.

No blink, no wayward
Glance, will interrupt your view.
Behold her ever.

See what gift death has
Given to you and your love.
See now what death does.

Do not cry out! No
Gods will hear voiceless prayers!
There's no divine aid.

Relax. See your love.
Know that soon your everness
Is Eurydice.

Sigh! Sigh! And breathe free.
Dream of hope and light and joy,
For in Hell they're not.

For Persephone,
Will not allow joy in Hell.
Will not allow love.

Arrogant husband
Die. See how Hell treats beauty
That's greater than mine!

Know that goddesses
Are generous, but also
That we are most vain.

Who's Eurydice
To be more beautiful, more
Loved than the goddess?

Greater than me? Is
She now? Then I will punish
Her love. Die! Die! Die!

Orpheus is dead.
Enter Eurydice, worn,
Torn, ravished, destroyed.

EURYDICE
Orpheus! You came.
You did not forget your love
To find another.

They tried to take from
Me my beauty, but I kept
All that's inside me.

Their claws could not touch
My soul. Their teeth tore, but did
Not mar who I am.

The Eurydice
You loved is still inside, though
Foul is the outside.

I will not speak of
The horrors they have done to
My outside, but will

Let you soothe my pain,
My hurts with gentle songs. Come
Dear Orpheus! Sing!

Come, Orpheus! Sing!
And bring gentle respite to
My great agony!

Look! See the beauty
Of which you sang such lovely
Tunes. Make me feel joy!

Come, Orpheus! Sing!
Had you not turned, I would be
Dancing in life's glades.

Come, Orpheus! Sing!
See the beauty. See her who
Is Eurydice!

Come, Orpheus! Sing!
Will you not honor our love?
Come, Orpheus! Sing!

Come, Orpheus! Sing!
Come, Orpheus! Sing! Dear love!
Orpheus! Orphe....

About the Author

Edward Eaton has studied and taught at many schools in the States, China, Israel, Oman, and France. He holds a PhD in Theatre History and Literature and has worked extensively as a theatre director and fight choreographer. As a writer, he has been a newspaper columnist, a theatre critic, and has published and presented many scholarly papers. He is the author of the young adult series *Rosi's Doors*, which includes: <u>Rosi's Castle</u>, <u>Rosi's Time</u>, and <u>Rosi's Company</u>. Other publications include the plays <u>Orpheus and Eurydice</u> and <u>Elizabeth Bathory</u>. In addition to his academic and creative pursuits, Ted is an avid SCUBA diver and skier. He currently lives and works in Boston, Massachusetts with his wife Silviya, a hospital administrator, and his son Christopher. Visit the author's website at: www.edwardeaton.com.

* * *

Author Notes

Orpheus and Eurydice was first staged by members of the English Language Theatre Group at the University of Nizwa, in the Sultanate of Oman, on 3 May 2010. It was directed by the author.

The cast was as follows:

Eurydice:	Emily al-Said Marriott
Orpheus:	Thuraya al-Nabhani
Persephone:	Amal al-Riyami
Hades:	Judy Darling
Demon 1:	Daria Rega
Demon 2:	Nada al-Manai

Muscat, May 2010
Boston, June 2012